"Closure" in grief
a mythical finish line

Brilliant Pongo

Published by Brilliant Pongo
Publishing partner: Paragon Publishing, Rothersthorpe
First published 2023

ISBN 978-1-78792-008-8

Book design, layout and production management by Into Print
www.intoprint.net
+44 (0)1604 832149

Prologue

There are just so many things often said to console or comfort someone grieving a loss of life. 'You must find closure' is probably the most confusing of all things said to someone grieving. I would argue it makes our grief so much more difficult. Friends and family have unrealistic expectations about what our grief will look like because of this myth. Indeed, trying to find closure in grief is akin to crossing an invisible line, a mythical finishing line that you are expected to not only find but cross.

Some people expect "closure" to occur following a funeral or memorial service, or after a loved one's room has been cleared out. Others seek closure after a personal ritual or the first anniversary. "Surely, we'll have closure then," we reason. We say a prayer.

But what a strange concept, closure....as if we could turn the lock and throw away the key, as if we could truly close the door on our emotions and love for someone who has passed away. Of course, the truth is far more complicated. In the realms of grieving the loss of loved ones there is no 'closure' it is but a mythical line that can never be crossed or reached.

The myth of closure is one of the most common of the many harmful myths about grief. How many times have we been told at funerals that we now have closure and can move on with our lives? As if a funeral will magically end the pain.

The notion that 'closure' exists – somewhere – sends us on an endless quest. We have no idea what it will look like or feel like; all we know is that we must have it. And if we don't find it quickly, something is wrong with us! Everyone tells us that once we have it, our grief will be over.

Avoid using this word if you are supporting a grieving friend. There is no closure! Take it out of your vocabulary. Grief, in reality, never ends.

It's something we'll remember for the rest of our lives. Some days, its weight may be so heavy that we are unable to get out of bed. Other days, we've put it in a small box on the top shelf of our lives out of necessity because we have to face the day. And then there are the times when it walks alongside us and a thought or a memory prompts it to speak up and remind us that it is there. This is loss. And it will never go away.

Closure may work well in practical situations such as business transactions and real estate transactions. However, closure does not apply to the human heart in its entirety. It is not possible to close the door on the past and pretend it never existed. And why would we want to in the first place... really? If we were completely detached from our loss, we would not only close the door on the pain, but we would also cut ties with our loved one.

When we lose someone close to us, we must remember that the relationship is not over. Death cannot take away the love that pervades every fibre of our being. In this regard, love will always triumph over death. We want to keep our treasured memories close to our hearts, acknowledging that our love is an essential part of who we are. In fact, we want to open rather than close the door on the reality of living with loss.

Perhaps it is better to abandon the concept of closure and instead focus on healing and growth. We can process our grief and progress to deeper and deeper levels of healing; we can find ways to move forward/on? while keeping our loved one's memory alive in our hearts; we can channel our grief into meaningful activities to honour our loved ones; and we can even learn to smile, laugh, breathe, and love again.

Our loss transforms love, transforming it from something that is dependent on physical presence to something purer. So let us not strive for closure. When we do this, we unintentionally close the door on all of the love we have shared. And, truly, that would be an unbearable loss, truly a tragedy.

Heck, sometimes some people cannot grieve in an organic way because they are pressured to 'get over' the grieving process and 'move-on' find closure-so-to-speak. Society has unrealistic expectations with regards the grieving process because of this myth 'Closure'. So, this book I set out to dispel the myth of finding 'Closure' in grief. In similar style to my previous book (Grief Sucks But Hope Again; a memoir of loss and pain) this book is also a memoir. I share from my lived experiences and delve into my grief journey.

1

What is 'Closure'?

For many in our society, closure means leaving grief behind, a milestone they usually expect to reach within a matter of weeks or months. Closure means being "normal", getting back to your old self, no longer crying or being affected by the death. It means "moving on with life" and leaving the past behind, even to the extent of forgetting it or ignoring it. Yet when we experience the death of a loved one, this kind of closure is not only impossible but indeed undesirable.

Closure, if one even chooses to use the term, is more of a process than a defined moment. The initial part of closure is accepting the reality. At first, you keep hoping or wishing that it weren't true. You expect your loved one to walk through the door. You wait for someone to tell us it was all a huge mistake. You just can't accept that this person has died, that you will never physically see your loved one again or hear the voice, feel the hug, or get that valued input on a tough decision. Usually, it takes weeks or even months for the reality to finally sink in. In time, you come to know, in both your head and your heart that your loved one has died and is not coming back. You still don't like it, but you accept it as true.

As you accept this reality, you can more actively make forward-looking choices that help you heal. You slowly begin to envision a life different from what you had planned before, a life in which you no longer expect your loved one to be there. You still feel the pain and loss, but except for short periods of time, you are not crippled by it.

Especially if it was a significant person who died, this healing phase is long and slow, and it involves a lot of back-and-forth-ing. You may alternate between tears and joy, fears and confidence, despair and hope. Sometimes you feel like you are taking three steps forward and two steps back.

Closure is now a central part of narratives of loss in realms like politics, media, and advertising, closure in some ways limits our empathy, failing to capture the varied experiences of many who grieve a death or other losses. The term is tossed around whether someone is recovering from a bad divorce or the death of a pet or trying to keep going after a natural disaster, terrorist attack, or shooting in their community. It's become a new, one-sized label for explaining what we need and how to respond after trauma, even as it's widely applied in a range of disparate conversations. Closure can be identified with justice, peace, healing, acceptance, and forgiveness as easily as it can be applied in conversations about unanswered questions or even revenge. Which is to say, far from the tidy finality it implies, closure is very confusing. It is a mythical line that try as we may, we can never truly cross.

A few years ago, my childhood friend Lucy who grew to be someone dear to me lost her mother in a tragic car accident. It devastated her life. We got even closer because her mother who was well known to me (she basically was my mother too) passed away just months after my wife's death.

Connected again by our grief, Lucy and I would talk of our pain and how to honour our dearly departed.

"This wasn't supposed to happen! Tell me why this has

happened!" These are the spoken words of countless bereaved persons throughout numerous years in numerous languages – a never-ending and always present wound in the Souls of those who have buried their loved ones.

Grief after loss of a loved one is forever boundless, an ever-present, deep-seated wound that has no name. There's a reason no label has been ascribed to those who have lost dearly loved ones – it is too foreign a concept, a much too chaotic form of brain freeze, an enormously frightening emotion for any language in the world to even consider naming.

Within that foreign concept lies the heart of the matter – losing a loved one is the most frightening, unspeakable, unresolvable, and ultimately the most devastating deprivation of a lifetime. It is disorienting, unimaginable, and is the most unacknowledged universal trauma of them all.

It is the very nature of this grief that makes the concept of "closure" almost laughable. Psychology tells us to look to closure as a way to live within this boundless grief. Finding the certainty, we need to make things whole again is supposed to exist within this concept so quickly spoken of by well-meaning friends and therapists.

The need for cognitive closure (NFCC) is supposed to provide us with an ending to all ambiguity and bring us certainty. Within that certainty, we should find freedom from all the questions that live and breed in our lives as to "why" our loved one had to die.

The problem is – most of those grieving because of death view their loved ones death as multi-factional.

It wasn't just the loved one who was lost; it was those surviving and grieving as well.

The bereaved lose their way in the world, and the entire

premise of how the universe operates is shaken to its core.

In the many conversations I had with Lucy, we explored the concept of closure and couldn't make sense of it. I began questioning the efficacy of this concept.

To me it was like chasing a shadow, a mythical line that could never be crossed.

Death may seem like a clear ending, but that isn't how it feels when you're the one up close to it. There's no clear finish line, because we can't comprehend the concept of death, the finality of it.

I remember Lucy saying,

"I don't want to 'move on' because I can't fully grasp it's real. I don't want to 'move on' because whether they're alive or not, they're a part of me.

I see my father in the black eyes that stare back at me in my reflection. I see him in the terrible jokes I tell. I see him in my love for reading, as he was the one who always bought me books. I see my mother in the way I treat people and how I expect to be treated.

I don't want closure from them because they are a part of me, they are my parents whether or not there are here to see me get older. I want to hold on to as many parts of them as I can, because I have way too little to last me over the years. I got 44 years with them; some people get more, and others get far less. But I am going to cling to those years and keep them with me.

You don't seek closure in grief because whether or not someone is here, they're a part of you, and you'll hold onto that.

This is actually a comforting thought, as my biggest concern was always losing them and moving on. It felt like that would be a betrayal. But now that I know that grief doesn't require closure". She said.

You find a place for your grief

In those conversations Lucy also spoke of finding a place for your grief as opposed to moving on.

"So instead of moving on, you find a place for your grief. You learn how to carry it best, to ensure that the weight of it doesn't pull you down but that you never fully let go of it. You find a way to honour and remember your loved ones.

I will always think of my father when I look at a beautiful sky. Whether it's a sunrise or sunset, seeing orange or pink shades in the sky will instantly make me think of him. I don't know if I believe about people still watching over you, but when I see the sky, I want to believe it's from him.

I think of my parents at the major milestones of my life. It's painful, to look around at birthdays or Christmas, and see that they are missing. But it's also a reminder to take a moment for it, to close my eyes and cling to their essence.

There is no need to find an end to grief, as it will accompany you until your final days. Instead, you simply find a place for it, a way to carry it without being consumed by it. You don't seek closure in grief, as your grief becomes a part of you as much as any other trait. I will forever be someone with grief. So, for now those around me will have to love me with my grief, as I don't come without it.

When did the concept of closure start?

The concept of closure, as applied to trauma and loss, took off in our popular culture during the 1990s. In the preceding three decades, cultural and political events had set the stage for this popularity. For example, the crime victims' rights movement, part of the broader "victim movements" of the 1960s and '70s, was instrumental in setting up scenarios and creating language that ushered in the political use of closure. Over time, many advocates in these movements used the concept of closure to help explain why victims needed particular resources or rights. Perhaps most prominently, death penalty advocates used closure for victims' families as an argument for capital punishment. By the '90s, court decisions began to reflect – and directly reference – victims' need for closure.

The past few decades have ushered in various other movements that focus on language about healing and closure, including self-help, pop psychology, and therapeutic jurisprudence. Furthermore, it is my view that the funeral industry plays a central role in popular understandings of grief because funeral home directors rely heavily on the idea of closure to sell their services. And, toward the end of the century, the concept of closure began showing up in news coverage of tragedies. One only has to look at America for example, how media houses such as CNN and Fox News covered cases such as Timothy McVeigh and the Oklahoma City Bombing, the Columbine school shootings, and the attacks of September 11, 2001. The news coverage angled and further popularised the concept of closure.

Hollywood has also packaged using the entertainment media to tell stories about crime, violence, death, and grief.

When traumatic things happen, as they inevitably do, people experience a kind of loss and they grieve over what has been lost – whether a life, relationship, home, or some other treasured part of life. In wondering what to do after such a blow, people might look to others; in many cases, they find cultural, religious, or family rituals to guide them through their grief. But if they do not have a strong religious or family tradition to follow, they may turn to other places – maybe even to a consumer culture that is ready to help provide rituals and meanings for those experiencing loss. Using closure to sell products and political ideas, salespeople and politicians become a potential resource for individuals trying to navigate a time of confusion and pain.

I remember the long conversation I would have with Lucy about how modern society and people in general viewed grieving as a linear process. How friends and colleagues expect you to shake off your grief and get back to normal.

Indeed, in these contemporary times, you may be led to believe that you need to achieve "closure" after the death of someone in your life. As a matter of fact, it is almost guaranteed to have someone approaching you and asking, "Have you had closure yet?"

In fact, "closure" as an end goal in grief is such a common misconception that many people have thoroughly internalized it. If we don't challenge this misconception, we are at risk for considering it a given – and we will no doubt struggle when we find that we're unable to cross the mythical finish line. Why aren't we reaching closure? Is there something wrong with us?

In the western societies, for a multitude of reasons – in part because of the need to try to put a happy face on things even when we should have proper sorrows of the soul, our lack of understanding of the role of hurt, pain, and suffering in the healing process, a desire for instant gratification, short social norms for mourning, lack of knowledge about grief and the need to mourn, and the inappropriate application of linear time-frames, we may lose patience with our grief when we really need to be self-compassionate.

So, closure is not some natural emotional state that we

can simply reach. Rather, it's a constructed concept, a cultural frame (how we translate our cultural and social experiences into explanations) for how we should respond to loss. Any understanding we think we have for this slippery concept of closure comes from how others have defined it through stories, arguments, court cases, and so on. This doesn't mean that the pain from loss or the process of healing is imaginary, but that how we respond to loss is shaped by our social world.

I have continued my conversations with Lucy as we navigate through grieving and finding ways to live with loss.

As Lucy was still trying to find ways to heal and deal with her mother's death, her father passed away almost a year after.

The feeling of having lost both parents becomes a life wound, a soul wound that never heals.

There truly is no definition for precisely what this form of grief feels like. It is a wrenching sadness and despair from which recovery cannot be found in what we call "closure."

Except that which somehow can reach deep within the recesses of what we know as Spirit and start a healing process – acknowledging that life isn't fair, we never really "get over" this kind of loss, we keep on breathing, and that parents do die.

Trying to accept our mortality and that of our parents, trying to accept all that has been or will be or can never be again, deciding how we will honour our parents or loved ones and keep them "alive" within our family, and trying to accept the fact that death is part and parcel of all life – may be the key to survival for those who suffer endlessly with questions for which there are no answers.

But there is never certainty, never total acceptance, and never closure in our collective human condition that keeps us from fully accepting all these things.

And, perhaps, an even more substantial impediment to consider can be found within one's need to "keep and maintain" the relationship with the loved one who has passed away.

Many times, holding onto the grief becomes the staple needing to maintain that relationship. As if letting go of the pain means letting go of the relationship – losing your loved one all over again.

Managing the connection within the grief experienced at the time of death can become all-important to a bereaved person.

Those final moments may be all that can be "felt" because anything else – memories of the good, the bad, and everything-in-between can become tangled up with unanswerable questions and lead to the could haves, should haves and if only-s of having no future with the deceased loved one.

Losing a future together can be often just as devastating as is the actual physical death of that loved one.

Even thinking of closure as a possibility then becomes some foreign notion that will never be considered because it is seen as a complete loss of all relationships – past and future.

Healing from the death of a loved one is a lifetime journey if there is any healing at all! And looking for "closure" does one thing and one thing only – it merely grounds you in the very thing that you are trying to heal within your very damaged and wounded Soul. I mean, life is hard stuff.

It presents itself in the light of day and the dark of night in varying shades of joy and despair-all on the same day.

Life is amazing. Then it's not. It's mundane. Then it's horrific.

You can't out-run it any more than you can defeat it. You can't change it without changing yourself, your environment, and your very Spirit. You can deny it and try to hide from the realities of it for a while until it catches up to you, which it always does!

Life can be messy and painful and joyful and filled with grief and laughter all at the same time. Don't try to plot it on a straight path; you will lose every time!

All you can do is look within and try to accept the mortality of all things. Then decide how you will be "in this world' and how you will honour those you love while trying to figure out how to accept yourself again.

Forgetting isn't an option. No drug, no mind-bending herb, no (as the song says) "wishing and hoping and thinking and dreaming" will take you back into that "before time." That moment in time is forever gone.

There is now only the "after time" to be dealt with and incorporated into what is remaining. What that "remaining" stuff is, well, that's up to the survivors to decide for themselves.

Take aways from this chapter:

1). Closure is not some natural emotional state that we can simply reach.

2). Any understanding we think we have for this slippery concept of closure comes from how others have defined it through stories, arguments, court cases, and so on.

3). The concept of closure, as applied to trauma and loss, took off in our popular culture during the 1990s

4). Don't try to plot life or grief on a straight path; you will lose every time!

2

There is no country with no grave – grieving is universal

I grew up in a very loving family and we loved music and dance. My father had a wide selection of music on vinyl record. We would turn the vinyl record player up on the weekends to play the records and we would dance and be merry.

One of my father's favourite record / songs was called (Hakuna Nyika isina rinda) by Flavian Nyathi and the Blues Revolution.

I never paid much attention to the lyrics at the time, I was drawn more to the rhythm of the music.

Loosely translated (Hakuna Nyika Isina Rinda) simply means there is no country on earth that has no grave.

The message was powerful and deep nonetheless accompanied by a danceable sungura/ jiti a very popular music genre from Zimbabwe.

The reason I bring this memory up is to show that each culture has a way of programming into us a way of accepting death nonetheless there are not as many ways that are then proffered on how to cope with or live with grief after the fact.

Indeed, we now live in a culture that avoids emotional discomfort. In fact, our society makes it easy to look for distractions and diversions from all things painful. If we can drink, eat, shop, TikTok or Facebook grief away, we will.

But here's the truth, we may have become accustomed to seeing and hearing about death. We may have attended a funeral (distant cousin or family friend) but nothing truly prepares you for loss of a significant other or loved one – losing a loved one is excruciatingly painful. And it doesn't just hurt for a few days, a few weeks, a few months, or even a few years. The impact of a major loss is lifelong.

Emotional "closure" is a cultural myth.

Why? Because no matter how many years go by – 10, 20, 30 – you will be changed irrevocably. You may think of your dear one almost daily and you will have days out of the blue that knock the wind right out of you. Certainly, the pain softens and eases over time. However, normal grief will always have moments of reoccurring sharpness, pain as raw as the very first day.

But consider this. If I suggested that I could wave a magic wand and make all of your enduring pain disappear instantly – with only one catch, that you would never have known your dear one... ever, they never would have been born – would you take that bargain?

No, you wouldn't. And you wouldn't because that relationship, that love, touched and enriched your life immeasurably. Your life without their physical presence is painful but your life having never known them at all is unthinkable. Their love was, and continues to be, a great gift.

Living with loss has no closure on pain but, thankfully, it also has no closure on love.

I was reminded of this on a trip to Zimbabwe. I went to visit with family in rural areas. What struck me was how close to the homestead the graves of the deceased loved ones are.

It is like they live right there in the compound/ yard.

My grandma's grave is a few steps from her kitchen. The graves are literally features in the compound, a part of the story side by side the dead are amongst the living.

Visitors go to these graves and literally speak to the dead. I found the experience very comforting, and I had an epiphany, indeed, an experience of sudden and striking insight into how life can balance and allow for a co-existence of loss and love.

While closure has a definition meaning finality. It means closing the door on something that has happened. It's a perfectly good word in the business community for closing a contract, for closing a real estate deal, or for closing a road and after a flood has occurred, but it is a harmful word in human relationships.

My people in Guruve (Zimbabwe) would not understand this concept of closure with regards death. Our dearly departed are only absent physically but they live with us.

Closure indicates that even though we have had attachment to someone once they are gone, we can close the door on them. That's not true for my people. There are continuing bonds as has been now declared in the grief literature. Nonetheless my people have always known and believed this, we don't close the door, we live with loss and grief. We transcend loss.

Transcending loss is the process of learning to live with love and loss side by side in a way that brings greater meaning and purpose into our lives.

My tips on how to do this simple, develop a practice of reflecting on the following three points and you will find that pain and love will become easier lifelong companions.

Loss is lifelong – Loss is our most universal experience.

We carry the remnants of loss with us every day. Let yourself grieve and feel your pain, riding the waves of feeling. While other people may tell you to "get over it," understand that "normal" grief never quite goes away. While it changes over time, its impact endures. Gentle acceptance of this fact allows you to begin to integrate loss into your life.

Love is eternal – You are still in a relationship with your dear one. This love is an integral part of who you are. Let yourself talk about your loved one, reminisce, look at photographs, and stay connected to this person who made such an enduring impact on you. Consider lighting candles in their honour on special days and/or giving gifts in their honour. They will always be a part of your life.

You are changed – Don't expect to return to your "old self." You are living into a new self. This self has new attitudes toward life, toward death, toward spirituality and toward your own life's meaning and purpose. Other people may have trouble with your changes but let them know that change is a natural part of living. Be open to new aspects of yourself coming alive. As you let yourself be changed, you will find that growth is possible.

Cultivating a more open position toward your grief will enable you to live with it more peacefully. Remember that after a death, love and loss go hand-in-hand. Closure on one would mean closure on the other. Fortunately, love is a benevolent force in our world that we simply cannot live without.

Take aways from this Chapter:

1). (Hakuna Nyika Isina Rinda) simply means there is no country on earth that has no grave.

2). Living with loss has no closure on pain but, thankfully, it also has no closure on love.

3). Cultivating a more open position toward your grief will enable you to live with it more peacefully.

4). Remember that after a death, love and loss go hand-in-hand. Closure on one would mean closure on the other.

3

Chasing the invisible line helpful or hurtful?

Three years after my wife's death I found the strength and ability to talk about her without feeling a flood of emotions that would almost always overcome me when I thought of her or spoke affectionately about her.

Although I knew what caused her death, I often found myself desperately wanting an explanation for her physical absence in my life.

There is something permanent about death, it is not like a relationship break up because when a love relationship breaks up. You can still reach out to your ex and seek an explanation to help you move on or find "closure" as they say.

I remember years back in my teens, I fell in love with a girl, my first ever love, it was in a beautiful border city called Mutare in Zimbabwe.

Young love can be so sweet, and the break-up can be terribly stressful and devastating.

Tatenda was my first ever true love (call it puppy love if you like).

Our relationship didn't last longer than a year we broke up for whatever reasons.

Not every couple that breaks up needs to cut off all

communication. Some couples are able to forge ahead with a friendship after some time has passed, especially after both have healed, while others do better if they never contact each other again. (Suffice to say 20 plus years on we still talk and are good friends).

That was my first experience of loss and I guess at that young age I did not know what to do, I was a novice at love and loss. Nonetheless, after the breakup I needed closure and strangely the one person who could give me comfort was the person who had broken up with me.

My first love now ex, (Tatenda) reached out to me months after we broke up under the guise of moving on. I recognized the same behaviour from her in myself – we both wanted to be comforted by the person who'd hurt us. Hindsight tells me we both wanted 'closure'.

Breaking up with someone is painful, whether you are the initiator or the injured party. Whether the reasons for breakups are frivolous and unnecessary or absolutely essential and irrevocable. It is never easy. Almost no one waltzes away from a breakup with a champagne glass in hand, toasting to their new life. Instead, the process of letting go is often slow and fraught with difficulty. Even new or shorter relationships can have an impact on your life, and the loss of a relationship as short as one month can present unique and difficult challenges.

I realized then that people often desire to "tie up loose ends at the end of relationships," though I'm not sure life works that way. Closure sounds like an appealing fix to all of life's messy problems, yet it may be the very thing holding us back from true peace. It's a question worth exploring: When is closure helpful, and when is it hurtful?

The need for closure doesn't just apply to relationships. The death of a loved one, the loss of a job, status or a way of life are other examples of painful endings. Letting go of something that was once important can be difficult, and many people seek closure in doing so. But does it actually help? And can you really expect other people to give you closure? Let's take a look at the evidence.

The social psychologist Arie Kruglanski coined the phrase "need for closure" in the 1990s, referring to a framework for decision making that aims to find an answer on a given topic that will alleviate confusion and ambiguity.

When we seek closure, we are looking for answers as to the cause of a certain loss in order to resolve the painful feelings it has created. In doing this, we appear to form a mental puzzle of what's happened – examining each piece and its relationship to the overall puzzle. Closure is achieved when we are satisfied that the puzzle has been assembled to our satisfaction, that the answers have been reached and it is therefore possible to move on.

Closure maybe found in broken relationships but there is no closure from loss after death

It's common to desire to reach out and find some sort of neat ending to complicated situations, especially when we didn't choose for a relationship to end. But the truth is, we're not actually searching for closure; we're searching for answers. And we want an opportunity to change the outcome of the situation.

We want to talk to that person again in hopes that they'll change their mind. Endings hurt and can bring up feelings of shame and insecurity. Sometimes, though, these feelings are part of the course when it comes to love and, well, life. It's up to us to choose how to move forward. It's vital to remember that we can decide how much we let the actions of others affect us.

I remember talking to my late sister about how my first ever love caused me heartbreak. In that conversation with my sister, I asked her why I let Tatenda break my heart and how she could hurt my feelings so deeply and made me feel so worthless? My sister replied that Tatenda was the sole cause. At first, I was incensed, thinking she was implying that Tatenda didn't do anything wrong. She went on to explain, however, that I decided I felt worthless, and I decided it was because of her actions rather than my reaction to them.

Recognizing that we have the power to make things mean or not mean something doesn't instantly take away the pain of being cast aside; it simply adds to a practice of shame resilience. My sister taught me something that has always remained with me, and it was that the "ability to recognize shame when we experience it and move through it in a constructive way is what allows us to maintain our authenticity and grow from our experiences." Actively looking to others for closure only prolongs the healing process. We have to find it within ourselves.

That teaching is truer, especially when the loss of a loved one is through death as opposed to a breakup.

Release Your Need for Answers

You may be arguing with me as you read through this chapter and page of this book right now about how some situations really do require a resolution. Closure is found for broken relationships but when it's loss as a result of death there are no answers Trust me; I get it.

As for broken relationships indeed, some situations are left unclear, and answers help us to understand how to move forward. Clarifying conversations can help us know what to improve upon or how to alter our course. However, we don't have control over how those conversations go or whether we can have them at all.

"Grief isn't linear and nuanced emotions are okay."

When it comes to estranged relationships or mourning the loss of a loved one, for example, closure can be an invisible line one hopes to cross. A mythical finishing line that one hopes to find with time. I felt this deeply at my wife's funeral service a few years ago. I loved her very much; I was very close to her. Her death left me confused, while her funeral service – full of tears, laughter, and love – brought me relief. She was an imperfect and complex human, just like the rest of us, so my complicated feelings about her were just fine. That felt like closure, but only because I was trying to manufacture it. Our faulty culture and our misplaced traditions and customs teach that after burial you find "closure".

I had already accepted that grief isn't linear and that my nuanced emotions are okay; the funeral service simply solidified that.

Closure is a mythical line we can't cross. The loss that comes as a result of Death of a loved one is not like a relationship break up. We can't white knuckle our way to acceptance and close a chapter on emotions that are yet to be written.

Most cultures and traditions teach us and makes us believe that if we try hard enough, we can get over our losses. We go to therapy and read books in an effort to find closure. We spend time with friends who help us move on from the breakup, the job loss, or the death of someone we love.

My burning question is what if we're going about that all wrong? With regards death, grief and closure? What if closure isn't actually good for us and in fact, stifles our normal (healthy!) grief process? What if moving on is a futile effort, because when something or someone has touched us so deeply that we feel loss when it's gone, it's a sign we need to keep that something or someone present in our hearts and minds?

Sometimes, when we have vulnerable conversations with those who have hurt us, it provides us a release. Other times, it confirms that we must learn to release on our own. Nonetheless, we shouldn't pressure ourselves to find an invisible line of closure.

Move Forward in Life

No one else is in charge of our happiness, no matter how much we wish they could be. But that doesn't mean we can't lean on trusted individuals to help us process our feelings. Reach out to a loved one, or a licensed therapist if you can, to help you unpack the situation with healthy dialogue and practices. Maybe the situation you're in is particularly difficult, and you need consistent support from others – don't be afraid to ask for help!

If you're not ready to reach out, try journaling about your feelings. No judgment from the page; simply let it out! Whatever you do, remember to practice self-care and gratitude because the future is undoubtedly bright, even if today isn't. You've got the power.

Take aways from this chapter:

1). The desire to have closure or resolution after the death of a loved one is part of our human nature.

2). We want explanations for the things we don't understand, and we find it difficult to move forward when pieces of the puzzle are missing.

3). When you don't have the answers you seek, it's easy to go into a downward spiral of sadness and despair. But the reality is that you won't always get answers to questions you seek, making it difficult to find closure.

4). There's no specific point where you'll stop missing your loved one. When you understand a few things about the grief process, you can help yourself, and others find peace after loss.

4

The need to know 'Why?'

If grief is a forest, then the death is its impossibly dark and winding centre. Many grieving people find themselves stuck in this centre, unable to move far past it, while others have somehow made it to the less dense, but still challenging, outskirts and refuse to look back.

If my characterization sounds bleak, I guess it's because this struggle is personal to me. Of course, I know many people have made peace with memories of their loved one's death and they can look back without feeling fear, guilt, shame, or intense sadness. Many have bought into this concept of 'closure' they say they have moved on but I'm not one of those people. I have come to terms with my loss. I believe that the concept of closure is akin to trying to run from your shadow. I choose to walk with my shadow.

In the three years since Tshidz's death, I believe my wish to keep her memory alive have been answered by learning to turn my "whys" into "how's."

Asking "why" isn't one of the official stages of grief, but maybe it should be. Anger and denial get all the attention, while getting stuck in the "why" freezes you in your tracks and prevents any opportunity for growth or movement toward healing.

Not being able to let go of needing to know "why" forces

you to focus on the rear-view mirror. It keeps you in the past and prevents you from living in a way that honours the person or thing you have lost.

It's in my nature to ask why. "Why" can be a powerful question that leads to clarity and progress. It can also be a roadblock in the one-way traffic of life.

Life doesn't come with reverse, only neutral and various speeds of forward progress. "Why" firmly plants us in neutral, and that's where I was in the months after Tshidz's death.

For me it was not necessarily about why she passed away it was more to do with family issues that arose after her death.

Many things were said which I covered in my previous book '*Grief Sucks But Hope Again*'.

The hate, the falsified stories some of which suggested we had divorced.

I couldn't make sense of the purpose of any of it.

I obsessed over the "why." My brain whirled at sonic speed looking for answers and a reason for these stories. I couldn't mourn or grieve in a 'proper' way (if there is any such way).

I assumed if I found the "why," I would find comfort and would be able to pick up the pieces and move on. I came up with elaborate theories of why her family was in attack and destroy mode.

Tshidz was home on leave from her job as a social worker when we got her prognosis of cancer but was scheduled to be back at work within the next few weeks. She was also due to graduate with a post graduate degree. She was excited to be a practice educator training other social workers.

I spun that into an even broader 'why'.

It made me feel bitter, but I was still left with the bigger question that would never be answered – why did it have to happen at all?

She was so dedicated to her job. She had worked long and hard to achieve her qualifications. She had been careful about her health and still the cancer came quick and gave her no chance.

All her hard work, all her plans her young son. It all was left. None of us had seen this coming. The doctors and all medical professionals had not detected this.

Asking the 'Why' question can sometimes haunt and suffocate you.

Death hurts, plain and simple. When someone who has touched your life passes away, it can feel like you've just lost a small piece of your world.

People often say that time heals all wounds. It doesn't heal them, but it gives us the opportunity to learn from them. Either we can learn from these lessons or ignore them and be challenged again and again until we do learn them. Grief teaches us to appreciate what we have and not to take it for granted.

When a loved one passes, your natural reaction isn't, "Hey, it's okay, this is a learning experience." Instead, it's instinctual to feel upset, angry, confused, hurt, hopeless. It often takes a little bit of time to accept this upsetting experience as one to learn from and that's alright.

The journey of grief has many points along the way. I have come to realise that from time to time during that journey, it's natural to find yourself wondering or asking yourself questions.

Oftentimes, these questions are predominantly the "whys?"

- Why did this happen to us/me
- Why didn't I do something sooner?
- Why did God let something like this happen?

"What's your why?" has become a motivational catch phrase.

"What's your why?" sounds absurd to the grieving person, and it's not comforting!

Not only had the "why" questions haunted me, I also found myself pleading with the universe for the explanation to "why this happened. "Why" is a question with no answer when it comes to loss. "Why" offers more questions than comfort.

Another word that isn't included in the official grief process, but again, I think it should be, is "how." "How" explores possibilities. "How" shines a light into the future. Exploring "how" to live a life that honours the memory of my wife made my wishes come true.

After realizing being stuck in "why" would never ease the pain of losing her, I began to realize that how I live the rest of my life is the outward manifestation of my wife's spirit.

- How can I start to feel better?
- How would she want me to move on?
- How do I find the positive in all of this?

I realised that I was going to be the vehicle of her legacy the only way anyone will ever get to know my wife, and the only way I can keep her memory alive.

If I continued to live in the "why," I would diminish her memory, but by living in the "how" I magnify her memory by my actions.

It doesn't make the grief go away; rather, it ignites my grief as a powerful vessel for change.

My "how" is manifested in cultivating a life of adventure and using radical self-care to ensure that I have the energy to embrace a life that reflects Tshidz's best qualities.

It is a labour of love for my wife that I embrace life, take risks, be courageous, pay it forward, and act in a way that makes people ask what I've been smoking. My actions are how I keep the memory of my late wife alive; it is how my wish has been granted.

If you or a loved one is stuck in the "why," let it go – it simply doesn't exist. It's time to live in the "how."

Take aways from this chapter:

1). Asking "why" isn't one of the official stages of grief, but maybe it should be.

2). "What's your why?" sounds absurd to the grieving person, and it's not comforting.

3). Grief teaches us to appreciate what we have and not to take it for granted.

5

Why closure is both important and problematic

"Closure" has become a buzzword for a commodity to be bought and sold.

Closure means many things to many people. It is a word used in diverse topics from medical procedures to computer programming, but I'm discussing a more recent use of closure that is applied to trauma and loss.

It is not the mere presence of closure as a concept that is a problem. The concern comes when people believe closure must be found in order to move forward.

Closure represents a set of expectations for responding after bad things happen. If people believe they need closure in order to heal but cannot find it, they may feel something is wrong with them. Because so many others may tell those grieving they need closure, they often feel a pressure to either end grief or hide it.

Many bereavement scholars, grief counsellors, and those grieving dismiss the idea of closure, but it continues to thrive in popular culture, politics, and marketing. Closure remains a dominant narrative about how to respond to a loss in large part because it's an effective political and marketing tool. The concept also fits most modern culture's quest to do things efficiently, following proscribed rules to get to a goal – in this case, an end to pain or loss. Since we are enmeshed in a consumer culture, it comes as no surprise that people turn to the marketplace to find grief rituals.

The 'closure talk' frames grief as bad and therefore something that needs to end. This rhetoric implies that closure exists and assumes it is possible, good, desired, and necessary. These assumptions (and the larger narratives that carry them) build feeling rules for how we are supposed to respond when bad things happen. Sociologist Arlie Hochschild introduced this concept of feeling rules – informal lessons we internalize about how to feel and express our feelings in specific situations – as a way to explain the consequences narratives have on people's emotions. We attempt to manage our emotions in different situations in an effort to look and feel the way we think we are supposed to look and feel in any given context.

This means there are problems when one's experience fails to live up to the promise of closure. For example, some death penalty advocates believe that after an execution, victims' families will be relieved and have a sense of closure. They argue that the pain felt when a loved one is murdered is so great that only seeing the same suffering on the part of the offender can bring healing. However, for many victims' families, executions leave only an emotional disconnect – they do not feel the closure promised.

Closure has become a neatly packaged concept used to sell services within the death care industry. It has been argued that in the 21st century, trends, like the rise in cremations have increasingly challenged funeral directors' profits. And thusly, the concept of closure has been packaged and pushed as a commodity by those in the funeral industry.

Take for example America which by many standards has hegemonic influence over the most part of the world. (What trends in American culture almost always ends up influencing other cultures)

In America, according to the National Funeral Directors Association, in 2009, 37 percent of deaths resulted in cremation as the choice for final disposition in the U.S., and analysts predict that portion will be 59 percent by 2025. This trend concerns funeral homes because they lose money if families choose cremation with no additional services: a typical cremation package costs $1,000-2,000, while a traditional funeral averages between $6,500 and $10,000.

Funeral home directors, then, need to convince people that at least some of their services are still needed even if cremation is the final disposition. This is where closure comes in. I found interesting examples that demonstrate or showcase this, DeVoe Funeral Services, Inc., located in New Jersey, highlights closure in their description of a funeral in this way:

"A funeral is an opportunity for relatives, friends, and neighbours to reflect upon and celebrate the life of the deceased and gain personal closure."

And Kohut Funeral Home (Allentown, PA) states on their website say the following:

"Viewing is part of tradition for many people who consider it part of closure."

As part of their marketing, funeral home directors sell embalming (not legally required in most cases, but funeral homes generally require it for a viewing) and a public viewing as necessary for people to reach closure.

Many people may choose embalming and a viewing and benefit from those services, but this does not mean they need those services or that they will lead to closure.

But the marketing by some funeral homes will tell you otherwise. Iowa's Hugeback Funeral Home characterizes cremations this way:

"The best-known option is 'direct' cremation. However, 'direct' emphasizes no viewing or visitation, no service, no casket or burial, and sometimes… no emotional closure for the survivors."

Other death care businesses promise closure through their services or products, including memorial soil (planting soil mixed with human or pet ashes), Teddy Bear Urns (stuffed teddy bears that hold small amount of ashes), or Life gems (diamonds made from a loved one's ashes).

Meanwhile, in most African cultures' cremation is not a preference and in many places it's not even an acceptable option. But elaborate tombstones and fancy graveyards are fast becoming memorialisation products sold to grieving families as ways to find closure.

Businesses in our world Sell Closure

There are a variety of businesses beyond the death care industry that use closure in their marketing. Many forensic pathologists sell autopsies using the concept. They claim that by acquiring additional medical information one can find closure to any questions about death or doubts about proper medical care.

Wrongful death attorneys use closure to sell the idea of suing others in order to have peace. Psychics tell people they can bring closure by talking to the dead to get questions answered or to know the dead are doing well. And private investigators claim that finding out what really happened – through their services – will bring you closure.

Companies selling DNA private profile kits promise "future closure" in the event you or a loved one cannot be identified after death. These same businesses sell paternity tests in order to find closure on questions about who fathered a particular child, and infidelity detective kits claim to help you find closure by examining your mate's clothes to see if he or she is having an affair.

The emerging "divorce party" industry uses closure to sell a range of products including cakes, break-up party invitations, cards, and divorce gifts. DivorceMagazine.com calls a divorce party "the coolest concept in closure."

Many businesses with break-up products adopt a theme of mock vengeance, selling items like Voodoo dolls, knife sets in the shape of an ex-partner, divorce cakes decorated with a murdered groom or bride figure, and Bury the Jerk kits and Wedding Ring Coffins to help you "bury the past."

Break-up party games, such as Pin-the-Tale-on-the-Ex and Penis Piñata, are supposed to playfully help you find closure.

Clearly, using closure in marketing has its appeal. For one, selling closure is a nicer, more comfortable idea that's easier to sell than straight-forward autopsies, embalming, expensive caskets, lawsuits, divorce parties, private investigations, DNA profile kits, and so on. These are difficult services to frame and market, but the emotional appeal of closure resonates with many people. I am not saying we should prohibit the availability of the products and services listed; I am however, saying it's simply deceptive and exploitive to promise closure in order to close a sale.

Politics, Too

As an ardent reader of politics and one that keenly studied

propaganda and media packaging. I felt it would be amiss to not bring in how this is used in politics.

Closure changes its meaning depending on the context and audience, which makes it easy to use in political arguments. The idea of closure provides a form of political shadowing: shining the light on closure and victims' pain and healing allows more politically cumbersome issues to stay in the shadows. For example, death penalty advocates claim that killing a murderer will bring closure to the families of homicide victims. They can use the more uplifting rhetoric of closure and therapy for victims in order to mask particularly difficult problems of capital punishment, such as racial and class discrimination, questions of innocence, and incompetent legal counsel.

Closure has even worked its way into legal decisions as a fundamental goal of law enforcement. The case for widening the scope of those who have to give DNA samples rests, in part, on the closure argument. Politicians say, "We need to collect DNA in order to provide closure for victims' families," and yet they rarely explain what that actually means.

Shining the light on closure and victims' pain and healing allows more politically cumbersome issues to stay in the shadows.

We know that victims' pain and healing are both important. But we should not lose sight of what is lurking in the shadows when closure is used as a political talking point. It may be a worthy discussion about whether to have a DNA database and whose DNA to collect. However, when the promise of closure is used to sell these political strategies, it distorts the grieving experiences of victims.

Following the death of Osama bin Laden, pundits declared that there could now be closure to 9/11. But many families of those who died in the terrorist attacks bin Laden's group perpetrated argued that his death did not bring closure because there is no such thing.

Following "feeling rules," we attempt to manage our emotions so as to look and feel the way we think we are supposed to look and feel.

It is not just in cases of murder where those grieving doubt that closure exists. Many people do not like the idea of closure because of what it implies. Individuals are different in how they interpret the concept, but here are some general reasons people give for dismissing closure: It is not possible because the pain never completely goes away. Closure is not good because it provides a false hope and not desirable because people do not want to forget their loved ones. And the language of closure is not necessary because there are other ways to find and describe hope and healing. Joseph Dougherty, who grieves for his brother, captures the frustration with this concept: "Closure implies finality, something ending or in completion. I challenge those of you who have lost a loved one to tell me if a single day passes when that person hasn't been in your thoughts, even if only for the briefest moment. Closure never occurs, because as long as all of us here today live, we will carry a part of this man in our hearts and our souls."

Bereavement research goes in different directions. There are scholars who say everyone's experience with grief is distinct and there's no specific timeline for grieving. Within this larger framework, there are theories for understanding grief that challenge the concept of closure, including meaning making and continuing bonds. The concept of "continuing bonds" explains that people who grieve often search for ways to stay connected with their deceased loved ones. Continuing bonds is a dominant perspective in grief research and contradicts most interpretations of closure but reflects the accounts of many who share their experience with grief.

From a different perspective, there are scholars who try to define criteria that measure some distinction between normal and pathological grieving, which shapes expectations for the "right" and "wrong" ways to grieve. This move reflects the medicalization of grief, which refers to a perspective that views grief as a disease that needs to be cured. Medicalization has led to language and grief models that set out proper ways to grieve within expected periods of time. Even though the word closure isn't a central component in this research, the framework for the medicalization of grief trickles down into popular culture. Most people are not going to be reading research articles, so short-hand descriptions are used to explain what "normal" grief looks like. Closure is often the short description of the "normal end stage" of grief, and the research criteria established for "normal grieving" get translated to "finding closure."

But the distinction between "normal" and "patholog-ical" grief is a construct, with researchers deciding (and not agreeing) on what belongs in the categories of right and wrong. Even though the expectations for "normal grieving" are constructed, they have real implications. On the basis of these criteria, people who do not fit the normal expectations or time-line for grieving might find themselves labelled as patholog-ical, abnormal, complicated, or chronic. Employers may expect bereaved workers to return to levels of normal productivity after a few days, while family and friends wonder why someone cannot find closure and move on.

Take aways from this chapter:

1). The distorted message about grief that comes from closure marketing is this: You need closure. Salespeople and politicians have entered the business of grief counselling, but their advice is rooted in profits and politics.

2). Selling products and politics in the name of closure exploits the emotional pain of grief, but it does not mean that closure exists or is needed.

3). Loss happens to us all. We grieve. Having a loved one die or facing another type of loss.

6

Don't get your head stuck in the grave

Life is a process of becoming. A combination of states we have to go through. Where people fail is that they wish to elect a state and remain in it. This is a kind of death.

When I was working on this book, I came across an image depicting a woman with their head buried in their loved one's grave. The image best explained what I tried to capture in my writing.

The term 'closure' is in my view an impossible line to cross with regards grieving the loss of a loved one.

Indeed, one can get closure after a relationship break up and job loss or anything other loss nonetheless when it pertains loss of a loved one to death it all becomes different. Closure becomes a mythical line we all chase and at times we even imagine we have crossed it.

From my personal experiences in the early stages of this journey after my wife's death, the best way I could put it, is that grief is like a fog – a thick, dense, and never-ending barrier between you and the world as you once knew it. The hope being the fog would lift, as fog tends to do, but after days and then weeks spent under its heavy cloak, you begin to wonder if it's become a part of your everyday life. In those moments, all you want and hope for is for things to feel better, "because you want to feel normal, whatever that may mean to you. Yet the simplicity of a 'normal' existence seems unfathomable. Impossible even.

Then, as time floats on one day, you look around and realize you can see a little further in front of you. Things are more colourful and they're coming into clarity. The days start getting a little bit easier, the nights a little more restful. The tears come a little less and things like laughter, joy, and gratitude and are once again a part of your emotional repertoire. The smallest sliver of light cuts into the dark and you realize that this must be what 'healing from grief' looks like. You also realize that progress doesn't feel as sweet as you had imagined. Something feels off," you say to yourself. "I should feel better about feeling better.

Over the course of time, it seems like love gets all mixed up with pain and grief. You realize your pain has become the expression of love lost – the way you honour your loved one, the one consistent link between life with them and life without them, and an element of proof that their life left an indelible mark on those they leave behind.

Apparently, while you were wishing the pain of grief away, it turned into something else entirely. In some ways, grief even becomes the way to define you in the context of life after loss. Who are you if you are not someone grieving the loss of someone very special? And who are they if you are not here, in life, holding vigil for them?

Your head remains stuck in their grave while the rest of your body tries desperately to continue with life.

Your mind is stuck in the 'what was state'. You function in the 'what could have been state' and avoid the present and now.

This could also be compounded by certain reminders of your loved one that are inevitable, such as a visit to the loved one's grave, the anniversary of the person's death, holidays, birthdays or new events you know they would have enjoyed. Even memorial celebrations for others can trigger the pain of your own loss.

Reminders can also be tied to sights, sounds and smells — and they can be unexpected. You might suddenly be flooded with emotions when you drive by the restaurant your partner loved or when you hear their favourite song.

I remember walking into an African shop local to our town, my wife was a regular at this shop the lady who owns the shop was very familiar to her. She would sometimes go there with my son. Months after Tshidz's had died my son and I went into that shop to pick up a few things. The lady recognised my son, and innocently asked, how is your mother, I haven't seen her in a while, pass my regards to her.

I froze and was tongue-tied. My son just looked at her and smiled awkwardly nodding his head as if to say 'I will' we walked out of the shop and did not say anything. I didn't know what to say to him. I was aware he was still trying to get to terms with his mother's passing and I was grieving as well. That reminder was out of the blue and caught us both unawares.

Remember, your loved one's memory does not live in the pain of your grief.

As cheesy as it sounds, your loved one's memory lives in YOU.

It lives in the stories that you tell people about your loved one. It lives in the memories you share together with friends and family. It lives in the things you do that your loved one taught you. It lives in the things you do in their honour and memory. It lives in every silly little thing you do to stay connected to them – from taking photographs, to listening to music they loved, to baking their favourite cake, to whatever other things you do to continue their legacy.

Now, it's easy to see why this reality might be confusing, because in the beginning many of the reminders mentioned above used to bring you a lot of pain. Things like music, photographs, and other reminders could easily spur an uncontrollable crying spell and endless hours on the couch eating whatever chewable comfort food. Reminders once equalled sad… So, it isn't a far leap to think that, if the pain starts to go away, these things mean less to you… Which means your loved one's memory is disappearing… Which means your love for them is diminishing.

But this is not what is happening, I remember having a conversation with a close friend of mine Sukii who lost her husband a few years ago. She told me about how she would avoid things that brought back memories that triggered sadness. I said to her 'but maybe it is because you have attached sadness to an otherwise happy memory, something that brought joy and happiness to you and your loved one needs not be triggering sadness"

Indeed, as humans we are capable of some amazing things, like resilience and adaptability. As time passes, your brain learns to manage the emotional pain and, slowly but surely, you get a little more control over the memory. As you get further from your loss, the pain starts to ease just a bit. What you must realize is that your loved one is not disappearing as your pain diminishes; rather, you are learning to live with the memory of your loved one in a different way.

Embrace the idea that as pain diminishes, you may actually

find more space to continue bonds and to keep your loved one's memory alive.

I remember months after Tshidz's died, as I drove to the gym Ariana Grande's song One last time, came on the radio in the car, I had to change the station immediately. It was too much; I was immediately emotional my eyes watering I ended up cancelling my gym session. This was her favourite song at the time it came out and she would sing/hum and butcher the lyrics out loud in the car. (Incidentally "One Last Time" was the last song that Ariana Grande performed on her Dangerous Woman tour stop in Manchester on May 22, 2017, minutes before the terrorist attack that killed 22 concertgoers in the foyer of the arena. This led to a fan-led campaign to push the tune to the top of the charts).

Now, when as that Ariana Grande song comes on the radio, chances are I will sing along, do a ridiculous car-dance, and tell whoever is around how much the song reminds me of Tshidz's.

Make a conscious decision to continue bonds.

Your connection to your loved one can be part of your daily life, even as you move forward and find a 'new normal' (I know some of you hate that term!). So, figure out what that looks like for you.

There will often be new and important people in your life who did not know your loved one. It may be new friends, a significant other, or children who never had the opportunity to meet your loved one when they were alive.

Find ways to tell new people about your loved one, sharing stories or photos. This is a way that your loved one's legacy continues, and you continue to keep them in your life as you move forward.

You may be surprised to see that, as you find positive ways to continue bonds with the person you have lost, you can let go of more and more of the pain without fear that you are letting go of the person you love.

Take aways from this chapter:

1). Life is a process of becoming. A combination of states we must go through.

2). Remember, your loved one's memory does not live in the pain of your grief.

3). Embrace the idea that as pain diminishes, you may actually find more space to continue bonds and to keep your loved one's memory alive.

4). Make a conscious decision to continue bonds.

7

Decluttering Sentimental Items and Keeping Memories

Decluttering sentimental items can be one of the most diffi-cult organization tasks. We all attach feelings and memories to objects, but when closets, drawers and cabinets start to over-flow with keepsakes, it's easy to lose sight of the truly special ones among a growing sea of clutter.

When you lose a loved one it can be difficult to let go of physical objects that hold sentimental value and memories.

I have a very vivid memory of things I did with Tshidz's the suits I wore to occasions with her.

The T-shirt I wore on our last walk/hike together and the collection of all trinkets like the last US-Dollar note we got as change on our last vacation together.

I don't know why I collected and kept these things, but I did.

Looking back now I see how I had become a closet hoarder.

It's hard to let go of items that we associate with loved ones or special places.

It is a complex thing really. On one hand it could mean the bereaved person 'cuts off' their grief, as to remember their loved one constantly is too painful.

On the other hand, it could help the grieving process by going through their belongings and remembering happier memories of the person, not just those linked to their death.

Nonetheless, I had to get rid of most of my clothes. Firstly, because they didn't fit me anymore. I dropped from a size 40 waist to a healthy 34. So there really was no reason to hold on to most of these clothes save it be for the memories I had attached to them.

We often want to keep things that remind us of loved one as a way of maintaining a bond with them. This is completely natural and understandable.

But sometimes this can hold us back and keep us in the mindset of them still being around. Sometimes when people finally get rid of the items collected, they can feel like a weight has been lifted and suddenly feel ready for a new start.

In my search for that mythical line of 'closure' I gathered keepsakes and almost hide behind myself in the clutter as it were.

The clutter that was in my mind had started manifesting physically in my room and gradually into the rest of the house.

Part of my healing from grief meant that I had to declutter.

In my opinion and from my experience I think the main challenges of decluttering when someone you love has died are threefold. First, in the state of grief and loss, it's really hard to untangle our desire to feel connection to that person with wanting to be surrounded by their stuff.

Second, it can be overwhelming for anyone to declutter their own lives. When you add another person's stuff on top and it can feel impossible to know where to even begin.

Third, we know the stories of our own things and that can lead to us being attached. But with our loved one's belongings sometimes we won't know what things are or if our loved one valued them, so we will assign value and importance to everything.

By getting rid of those things that I had held onto as keep-sakes I freed up space not only physically but mentally and emotionally to process and accept my grief and learn to truly accept that I don't physically need constant reminders of my wife.

The memories are mentally engraved and that is the best place to store all experiences. I only need a few physical things. I had to declutter I got rid of all things I didn't really want and now I can truly enjoy the objects that bring out the best memories.

Setting on a chest of drawers in my bedroom is a candle that I got from Tshidz for the last Father's Day she shared with me I found it in all the clutter on the day I threw out most of the stuff.

"Husband without you I'm nothing, with you I'm some-thing, together we are everything."

A poignant message that I cherish and hold dear.

Indeed, it can be stressful and difficult to declutter and get rid of sentimental objects.

But a dear friend recommended a way to help do this. She said to me ask yourself three questions when taking stock of your sentimental clutter.

- If you had to purchase the item yourself, at full price, would you?
- If someone you don't like gave you the item as a gift, would you still keep it?
- Does the item evoke happy memories?
-

She said to me if you answered no to more than one question, you should get rid of that thing. To avoid feeling guilt, my dear friend said to me remember that "you're not giving away the person, the love of that person, or that person's love for you."

She added that you shouldn't keep an item if you can't identify a clear reason for why you are keeping it.

And with that wise counsel I was able to get rid of a lot of clothes and trinkets that cluttered my room.

Indeed, everything we own is a time machine. I guess as humans we like to revisit the past because we are wired to think it was a better time, but if you focus on what's behind us, we're not present enough to create new memories, which could leave us quite melancholy.

You can ditch the item without ditching the memory.

Many people hold onto stuff left to them by family members, even if they don't have room or want it. Ask yourself, would your relatives want this stuff to weigh you down? If you're not using it, its just clutter. You can love and remember your family (and they'll still love you) without keeping physical stuff which in most cases is just clutter.

Everything you own should make you feel good.

This seems obvious, but things get tricky when it comes to sentimental items.

I had for a while kept my late wife's journal, and when I'd get depressed or angry, I'd look up dates to see if certain days were important to her. Sometimes, I would go to places we previously went together, and I would feel so sad, and it would bring tears to my eyes. But I came to a realisation that this was not how I wanted the stuff I hold sentimental and the things I keep in my home to make me feel. And so eventually, I was able to get rid of the journals and all the little trinkets.

Instead of hoarding items in boxes, display a few pieces from an overgrown collection to satisfy your sentimental side.

I proudly display my candle with a beautiful message in my bedroom. It is a living thing now, and not just dead energy.

A few days after clearing out my room I came across this quote during my morning reading and it made a tone of sense: 'The barn's burnt down, now I can see the moon,' In light of what I had got through a few days prior with the decluttering exercise it became my quote of the week

Remind yourself that you're not casting memories and heir-looms to the side – you're creating breathing room in your current life, freeing yourself of extra weight, and recognizing that what's most important is happening right now – not in a box in your attic or trinket collection under your bed.

Decluttering' after a person dies can be a difficult and even upsetting experience, but it can actually be part of the healing process after losing a loved one.

Take aways from this chapter:

1). Decide if you're at a place in your mourning and grief where you are actually ready to begin decluttering. It's ok if you aren't. Be kind to yourself and take your time.

2). Start with your own belongings. This really serves as a warmup. A chance to experience decluttering in a less emotion-ally challenging area.

3). Choose a few of your favourite, most treasured items of

your loved one. Give these items places of honour in your home and display them in a way that brings you joy and helps you feel connected to your loved one and their memory.

8

What is time's actual role in healing?

If you ever thought that all you needed was a few months to get over something traumatic, trust that you are not alone. Most of us have been there and believed the same thing before. After all, the popular cliché "time heals all wounds" is used by many people for good reason.

However, Time in itself – unlucky for us – does not heal all wounds. I think it was Lilly Tomlin who said, "tragedy plus time equals comedy." There's something to that. We can all look back at certain hard or painful situations in life and laugh now about them. But the main point is time is just a concept we use to measure minutes, days, hours, months, years.

In truth Time is not a healer. The passage of time may take the edge off of acute pain, but it does not heal pain. On the other hand, time can be used well for healing purposes. When time is used well, in terms of healing wounds, then it is because we do something specific with and within it. We take time and shape it in order to do inner work. It is inner work coupled with courage and honesty that heals all wounds.

Healing wounds of grief, can time do it?

Ever notice how painfully slowly time moves when you're sitting injured in a hospital? Or when you've got a migraine, or tooth ache and you're waiting for the painkiller to kick in? The same rules apply when you're in emotional agony.

"Time heals all wounds" is like a slap in the face when minutes feel like hours, hours feel like days, and the days, feel like months.

It sounds absurd to imagine a doctor looking at a broken leg and saying,

"Time heals all wounds," or "Give it some time."

Yet that's exactly what people say to grievers.

Time is certainly an important factor when it comes to healing. Although it may take away some of the pain, sorrow, or other negative emotions associated with an experience, time on its own is not a healer.

Whether you are going through a breakup, grieving the loss of a loved one, or going through something else emotionally taxing, plenty of other important factors are involved in the healing process.

Indulge me as I try to point out why the cliché that "time heals all wounds" may not be fully true, as well as time's true role in healing, other factors involved, and where you can focus your efforts to speed up the healing process.

Time's Role in Healing

What is time's actual role in healing? I would put it to you that time essentially equates to opportunity. Therefore, how someone heals over time ultimately depends on how they decide to use that opportunity to shape their present and future circumstances.

Indeed, people can use time to gain insight, healthier relationships, and an orientation toward growth. Some people will use time as an opportunity to collect experiences that orient them toward their values and dilute or challenge difficult experiences.

I remember talking to a friend who was concerned about her sister, they had just lost their mother and her concern was that her younger sister did not seem to be mourning or grieving (in ways she thought would be normal) but was somehow focused on having fun and drinking making jokes and living as if their mother had not died. There is what I would call an unwritten rule in some societies that forbids any form of fun and laughter from those grieving or mourning. They are somehow expected to be extremely sorrowful and be tearful.

I explained to her that perhaps this was her younger sister's way of grieving. It could have been her way to dilute or challenge a difficult experience.

We all have an idea of how grieving goes, and unless we have our own experiences, they're often a mishmash of assumptions gathered from movies, pop culture, and anecdotes. Often these simply involve lots of crying. It's rare to see an accurate representation of angry grief or numb grief, but they're very common experiences, too. Even when we have our own experiences, they may not be that useful when we're attempting to understand or comfort someone else. Because although all grief shares some key similarities – it hurts – each individual person's grief is different.

Ask many people who have suffered a significant loss, and they'll tell you that the initial shock and pain – while agonizing – wasn't the most difficult time for them. That may come weeks or even months later, when the reality of life without a loved one begins to set in (and those who supported them through the early days of the loss take a step back). The sense that you can never, ever speak with this person again – never touch them, hear their voice, or feel the unique way you did with them

– has begun to sink in.

So, time may, indeed, heal you, and probably will, even if it's not a straight road. But what that healing will look like, how long it will take, and what you will think and feel and do and experience along the way, nobody can say. Your grief is yours, and nobody can tell you what will happen. I imagine that is both a comforting and disconcerting thought. But then again, perhaps not.

Time is a 'healer'?

The "truth" of the statement, even when it is true, depends entirely on what you mean by "heal."

We often talked about the nature of time, and how it heals. But we seldom talk about the nature of wounds.

Indeed, we must ask ourselves what particular kind of wound is a major bereavement, and what would it look like when it heals?

Are we talking of a cut that heals completely? A nasty burn that will always look a bit mottled and weird. A deep gash that leaves an ugly scar. An amputation?

When you have a physical illness or an accident, everyone can see that something isn't right. When you're grieving, nobody can read it on you, nobody can see that you're wounded. Grief is an invisible wound. You look in the mirror and see the same person but at the same time you almost don't recognise yourself because you feel so different inside.

All of us are recognisably human beings but we're also very different, with our hair colour or eye colour. It's the same with grief – we're different emotionally and psychologically in how we process pain on the inside.

How we experience grief and loss and how we process it will have lots of invisible components: our upbringing, our previous history of loss, the support we have at the time of the loss, the circumstances of the loss, and the relationship with the person that died. All of this is invisible.

Time also allows for reflection on the difficult experience in a way that promotes insight and the ability to make positive progress when dealing with grief.

So why do people say time heals grief?

In my opinion people use this cliché maybe based on the common perception and understanding that the intensity of your feelings might decrease over time, but that doesn't mean time alone is what's doing the healing. It's what you do within a particular time frame, the action you take, that will help you move-forward in the emotional grieving process.

Nonetheless, it is my take that when you force-stop your grief or pause it/ avoid it and not allow yourself to walk through/process it. This in turn limits your capacity for joy and happiness. It limits your ability to function in the world and to be fully open to connecting with other people and experiences. That's no way to live.

If you're grieving a loss, it's time to stop waiting to feel better and to take action. It will require courage and an open mind. You owe it to yourself. When you wait remember time is ticking on it won't stop for you or anybody.

What Can Prevent Healing?

It's possible (and highly likely) that time will not heal all wounds for several reasons. So, what can prevent someone from healing as time goes on?

In my view the following things may prolong your healing, even though a notable amount of time has passed:

- Remaining fixated on something, like how a loved one died
- Refusing to let go of a betrayal by holding a grudge
- Denial that something has happened
- Not having a solid support system or emotional outlet to express your emotions
- Resorting to unhealthy coping and/or distraction mechanisms
- Relying on drinking or taking drugs to numb pain associated with the event

In addition to ruminating, people can use time to support the limiting beliefs that they have that keep them stuck in a cycle of negative experiences.

[They] find themselves stuck and living in the past as though no time has elapsed after the experience of a difficult event.

Of course, some experiences are so traumatic that they leave us scarred for a while, and this scarring is our brain's way of keeping us healthy.

How to Promote Healing

Some factors differentiate those who move on with time and those for whom time seems to provide the opportunity to become more entrenched in a loss, trauma, or other difficult experiences.

Essentially, how you utilize your time is directly correlated to how well and how quickly you will heal. So, let's take a look at some factors that help facilitate the healing process.

Integrate Lessons You've Learned

People need the opportunity to express their pain in ways that marry insight and emotion. This could mean creating art based on your experience, making music, creating journal entries, or writing stories. Ultimately, you can express your pain in a way that feels cathartic and healing to you, so it doesn't stay bottled up or turn into an unhealthy expression down the line.

Honour Your Emotions

Give yourself grace to fully process your emotions. This is especially important after experiencing a traumatic situation, like death. Release any judgment associated with the experience and allow yourself to accept and feel whatever comes up for you in order to move past it.

Receive Support

Spend time with those you trust who can offer you emotional support in your time of need. This can be friends or family.

Align Your Actions with Your Values

Pursue the hobbies you enjoy and make new memories doing what you love to help yourself achieve a deeper sense of healing.

Techniques to Speed Up the Recovery Process

Instead of solely depending on time to heal your wounds, there are other areas that you can focus on to promote healing. To achieve a deeper sense of healing, you can:

- Spend time with loved ones
- Connect with new potential friends and partners
- Journal
- Meditate
- Improve your physical health

- Collect new experiences (e.g., travel, meet new people, etc.)
- Practice gratitude for all of the positives in your life

What are your chapter take aways?

1).

2).

3).

4).

9

Moving forward, not moving on

"Moving forward" or "moving on". They sound like such similar phrases, don't they? But in the context of grief the difference between "on" or "forward" is huge.

When you're grieving for a person who you love – people will often say things like, "Isn't it time you moved on?" or "You'll move on eventually" or even, "I'm glad to see you've moved on".

But the idea of moving on from a loved one can be incredibly distressing.

Moving on implies leaving something behind. It suggests that your loved one who has now passed on, for example, or the places and memories that you shared and cherish can be put behind you when, in fact, he or she was a member of your family and you'll never get over that loss – not in the way that moving on implies, anyway.

My hope is to encourage people to shift how society approaches grief. Too often, people think it's as easy as moving on, but this is one of the many myths about grief. We don't just move on. We don't simply forget and move on. Rather move on from our grief, we must instead find ways to move forward with it.

We must as a people, as society try to remind one another that some things can't be fixed, and not all wounds are meant to heal. We need to help each other remember, that grief is this multitasking emotion. That you can and will be sad, and happy; you'll be grieving, and able to love in the same year or week, the same breath. We need to remember that a grieving person is going to laugh again and smile again… they're going to move forward. But that doesn't mean that they've moved on.

The connotations of "moving on"

While people who haven't experienced grief might like to think it has an endpoint, those of us who have lost someone we love, know that there is no cut off point for our feelings.

Grief doesn't come with a timeline, whereas the phrase "moving on" suggests that it does.

Other vocabulary people use can suggest the same thing. You might have someone say to you, "I'm glad to see you're feeling better now" or be party to a conversation in which someone says, "I don't think they ever got over the loss of their < loved one>". People often talk about "closure", as though you can simply close the cover on the book of grief.

Such phrases imply that there will come a moment when the grief is done and dusted. When it isn't, it can make us feel like there's something wrong with us. But there truly isn't.

We don't move on from grief

Following the loss of a loved one, it's important to remember the grieving process has no set timeline. We don't just grieve the moment they pass and move on. Instead, we grieve the past and present. We grieve what could have been the future. This is because our loved one is more than just one moment in time.

We can never truly move on from grief, only forward.

"Moving forward"

It is far more compassionate and realistic to talk about moving forward after a bereavement.

When a loved one dies, our love for them is still very much present. We expect them to be waiting for us when we get home or listen for the sounds of them moving around like they always did. We slip into the present tense when we talk about them because we think about them all the time and they will never just be left in the past.

After all, it was our loved one(s) help who to shape us and so they are forever a part of our identities.

You would not be the person you are today without the loved one you have lost. You made memories together, felt joy because of them, built your life around them.

How can you move on from someone who has fundamentally changed you?

Inevitably though, we do have to find a way to move forward.

As much as we can feel frozen in our grief, life will keep moving and we are left with no choice but to find a way to live in the world without our loved one.

But it isn't that our grief eventually shrinks, it's that we learn how to grow around it.

For many bereaved people, the idea of moving on or forgetting is one of the most problematic parts of grieving. As Dr Tonkin aptly puts it in her model that it is okay for grief to always be part of your life.

In essence, Tonkin's model of grief challenges the idea that 'time heals all wounds' or that grief disappears with time. Indeed, if you have recently lost a loved one, you might feel as though it is impossible to ever move on from grief. Dr Tonkin suggests that this is because we do not move on from grief but grow around it.

Dr Tonkin's model of grief suggests that grief actually remains as big and present as it has always been but, with time, your life will begin to grow around it.

Growing around grief

Imagine drawing a circle to represent yourself. This is you, your life and everything you're experiencing. Now you shade in the circle to represent your grief.

The result is a circle, almost entirely shaded. This is you and your grief; it may be entirely consuming your life. You may feel unable to eat or sleep or find yourself struggling to think about anything else.

What happens in the following days, months and years is important. Rather than the shaded area growing smaller, the outer circle (representing you) begins to grow bigger. The result looks somewhat like a fried egg, with the white representing your life and the yolk representing your grief – this is why this model of grief is sometimes referred to as the fried egg model.

Tonkin's theory of grief suggests that over time, your grief will stay much the same, but your life will begin to grow around it. You will have new experiences, meet new people, and begin to find moments of enjoyment. Slowly, these moments may grow more frequent, and the outer circle will grow a little bigger.

Eventually, there will be a much larger circle, with the same size shaded area – but the grief is not as dominant overall. This is why Tonkin's model of grief is called growing around grief.

This does not mean the grief disappears. It will probably always be there and may even grow a little bigger at difficult times. But it no longer completely dominates the circle.

You will experience new things, meet new people, have new love, learn new skills, visit new places, enabling the space around your grief to get bigger. This is the process of moving forward.

Grief isn't an either/or emotion. It's not that you feel grief and nothing else.

In fact, grief can be present while you experience other emotions too. You can be grieving and still experience joy.

I remember talking to a security guard who comforted me when I broke down in a shop, (I never got his name) but I remember his counsel he said to me "it's okay to cry, it's okay to grief painful as it is now you must remember that grief is just love that has nowhere to go".

How true.

If we believe this, then we can move forward knowing that grief is the locket that holds our love inside of us.

And maybe that's a special thing, to have a love that we carry always. Why would we want to "move on" and leave love in the past when we can move forward and hold it with us forever?

However, as a parting note for this chapter you should bear in mind that Dr Tonkin's model of grief that I explored is only a theory of how grief works. There are many other models of grief which may more accurately represent how you experience grief. Everyone is unique in how they react to the death of a loved one and none of these models represent the 'right' way to grieve.

Take aways from this Chapter:

1). There is a huge difference in moving on and moving forward as far as grieving and grief are concerned.

2). Too often, people think it's as easy as moving on, but this is one of the many myths about grief.

3). For many bereaved people, the idea of moving on or forgetting is one of the most problematic parts of grieving.

4). Grief isn't an either/or emotion. It's not that you feel grief and nothing else.

In fact, grief can be present while you experience other emotions too.

10

No way round it

It's the question often asked; How soon after the loss of a beloved partner should someone start a new relationship?

When you experience the death of your spouse, it's natural to feel the effects of that loss manifesting in loneliness and the need for human companionship, especially if the loss is sudden. Seeking love and attention in another person may help fill in the hole that your spouse left behind when they died.

The fear of entering into a new relationship

Quite apart from the judgements and opinions of others in these situations, our own emotions can be really confusing, and we can be quite vulnerable while going through the grieving process. These factors can make it even more of a minefield than relationships are at the best of times.

Count it as fortunate to find someone who understands that you loved and will always love your deceased spouse and they are completely comfortable with it.

This is the dichotomy of the human heart.

We think our hearts should, and must, permanently close before opening to someone else. Don't we?

We cannot think or even assume the position to be in a new, loving, open, thriving relationship if we love someone else, can we?

We are not supposed to "move on" into a new love if we

haven't set the love down and walked away from the old.

False.

I am proof we can.

I love my late wife, still. She has been gone for couple of years, and I miss her, I love her. All the time. Every day. And I also deeply, unconditionally love my new blossoming relationship with my girlfriend. It's that simple. And it can be. I love her, and I love Tshidz, too.

Unfortunately, sometimes as people grieving, we diminish ourselves and the capabilities of our hearts and spirits when we suppress our love and loves and hide them away. Specifically, if we are grieving for a lost love and a lost life as we knew it. Look at what your heart is capable of giving and doing and give it credit.

Love is a superpower, and we all possess that superpower.

Your superpower is loving harder than any pain you have ever felt, and you probably had no idea you carried that around with you.

I certainly did not know, nor did I comprehend this. It was some time after wallowing in grief that I realised I have much to give, lots of love to expand.

If you've ever had to deal with loss of a spouse, and you're still here to talk about it, you have flexed that intrinsic capability. We were powerfully made to love, hurt, heal, overcome, expand and love again. The one who loves urgently after a loss has glimpsed their heart's true potential.

Our hearts can and will do what they were intended to do: expand. And allow more love to be given and received. So let them.

The greatest gift we can give ourselves, and the ones we choose, is permission to love all. Honour and cherish all the lessons in the love(s) we have had and allow that wisdom to bring our best to the new. We have collected all the data we need to level up in the new relationship.

One of the greatest lessons that my walk with grief has taught me is that we can keep my heart closed and compressed by denying my emotions. But that is a form of self-abuse if not punishment.

I have the option to do the opposite, I can as I have done let myself fall in love and keep loving, it will benefit me and make me whole again.

Although I have experienced a tragic loss and might grief for as long as I have memory.

The love I have for Tshidz is frozen, unable to grow and flourish. Growth has ceased. But I take comfort in knowing perhaps believing that I am able to admire that flower for the entire lives, but no new love will grow or root further there. I have accepted that she is gone. I am new. And thus, I am establishing a root system and with patience, grace, understanding, I will in my new relationship grow and nature all the tender love and care and continue to bloom.

The best thing I can do for myself and perhaps in Tshidz's honour is to be happy and to love again like I've never been hurt. Bring all the knowledge of your history into my new love and do my best and be the best version of myself.

The gap left by a deceased spouse sometimes allows us to tap into a new depth of love, one we didn't know existed. It feels like a depth we simply couldn't access prior to grieving. It is a type of love predicated on the void they left in your (love) world.

When someone dies, their absence becomes its own presence. We come to love and hate that void. It represents all that is gone, all that we loved, all that we miss. We hate the reality it represents – that they are physically missing from the world. But we also love the reality that it represents – that our love for that person is so great that they are still "here", even when they are no longer physically here. We grab a-hold-of their absence/ memories and cling them as tightly as we can. We still visit and revisit our lived and shared memories, knowing they hold both the deepest joy and the deepest pain. We marvel that the depth of our love, our loss, and our grief. We want the grief to end, and we want it never to end, all at once.

With their absence, we learn something we couldn't know while they were living. We learn just how deeply we were capable of missing them. We learn just how much pain their void in our lives could cause. We learn how willing we are to lean into that pain in order to keep them close. Though we can imagine what it will be like to lose someone we love, when it happens, we learn it was actually unimaginable. And in that gap between what we imagined and what we never could have imagined, lies a type of love we meet for the first time in our grief.

To those you have been hurt either by death of a spouse or break up.

Open the space in your heart that has been wronged or betrayed… and let that all go. Create heart space by letting go of what doesn't allow you to expand. Take ownership of being your best, with the knowledge you have, and enter into the new love with an open and elevated heart and mind.

Nothing can hurt you if you don't allow it to. Create space in your head and heart by letting go of what holds you hostage from healing. Then, you'll be able to open and expand. And watch as you and your person bloom.

The strongest and most courageous hearts are the ones who

know they're capable of loving all, honouring all, and giving their all because of it.

You don't take away from the new love by acknowledging what love(s) brought you to the present one. Be brave and honour it all.

Whether you are grieving the death of a partner, or the loss of a loved one, there are many questions and issues which can arise when you meet someone new and fall in love.

If you have had a happy relationship and experienced love, in my view, it is a compliment to your partner if you want to experience that again. The love for your lost partner will be ever present, but as I have said before our human hearts are capable of unlimited love and have room for future relationships. No two relationships will ever be the same, neither will the love of your new partner be the same as for the person you lost. But you can be happy again. It isn't dishonouring the deceased to love again. They would have wanted you to carry on, make the most of your life and be happy again.

Take aways from this chapter

1). The gap left by a deceased spouse sometimes allows us to tap into a new depth of love, one we didn't know existed.

2). Love is a superpower, and we all possess that superpower.

3). The one who loves urgently after a loss has glimpsed their heart's true potential.

4). The gap left by a deceased spouse sometimes allows us to tap into a new depth of love, one we didn't know existed.

11

To love both; one here, one gone

It's sad but true: Many people who have faced the loss of a partner way before they ever expected can still find love. It is possible to love again and be in a fruitful healthy relationship after loss. Once the dust settles (so to speak), some people jump back into the dating world right away, while others feel like their grief is still too strong for many years afterward.

Indeed, we all have romantic predicaments; widows (and widowers) seem to have even more. Should they actively search for another lover? And if they find another lover, while still loving their late spouse, how can these two lovers reside together in their hearts? For some who have lost a spouse, the predominant question is, is loving again worth the effort of having to adjust to another person? And is there a proper time to fall in love again?

You are not destined to remain in mourning forever ... that isn't why you are here.

Challenging as it maybe for those grieving the death of a spouse. I personally would encourage you to embrace and carry forward the legacies that were entrusted to you by your late beloved. If you choose it, living your new life can include companionship ... and love.

Indeed, grieving the loss of your partner doesn't actually mean you're not ready to date or find love again. In truth one never gets over major life losses – meaning you will always feel something. To me, this is beautiful and in no way means a widow or widower shouldn't move on and form other bonds.

Though every person is different, if you've given yourself some time to grieve and to honour the relationship, you're ready to get back out there (you don't move on but move forward). In fact, it could make your next relationship even better than you imagined.

Many people experience loss as a heart-opening experience: You learn to love deeper, savour what you have, and use any regret from the past relationship to learn, I would say.

Nonetheless, depending on age some people choose to remain single as widows or widowers.

Maybe because they struggle to accept a new love in their life because they believe they loved their first partner so much that they could never love again.

But I believe it is possible to find love again and have a fruitful relationship. It is possible to find someone that accepts that as a widow or widower you have a past, you have some who will be mentioned in the course of the relationship. Anniversaries, birthdays and other memories that will be important to you and will need to be honoured.

I strongly believe that the human heart is large enough to encompass more than one romantic love. There is ample evidence that this is possible, both in the diachronic sense of loving one person after another and in the synchronic sense of having two lovers at the same time. Widows' and widowers love indeed involves both aspects.

I have experienced second love after my wife's death and I can with hand on heart attest that it is different, but it's very good. I will always love and miss my late wife. It's really hard to understand sometimes how I can go from tears for my late wife into smiling and thinking of my new lady. There's an odd 'divide.' I love both of them, one here and one gone." It seems that we are blessed with a heart that is very flexible and can accommodate various people at the same time.

For some widows and widowers, your love for two people is more complex given the continuing impact of bereavement, even years after the loss. As a widow or widowers', the ongoing relationship and bond to the deceased may remain a central aspect of your life. You have to cope not merely with the new situation of loving two people at the same time, but also with the shift in the way you have loved your deceased spouse: a shift from a relationship with a physical companion who provides active support and love to one who is no longer alive and cannot be active in your life.

Connecting the dots to closure

So how is this all connected to the topic of closure in grief after the death of a spouse? Well, the point I have laboured to make here is that when it comes to grief after a loss to death 'closure' is a mythical line that cannot be crossed.

Indeed, there is a difference in the case of a widow's/ widower's love for a new person from that which pertains when a regular love affair occurs after a previous one has ended. This is especially so if, at the time of the spouse's death, both part-ners shared a profound love. In this case, the survivor's love does not die with the spouse's death.

The love felt for the late spouse is likely to increase in light of the prevailing idealization of the relationship and of the spouse. Although a new love might physically replace the previous one, from a psychological viewpoint, the widow/

widower will now love two people at the same time. Their love expresses the nonexclusive nature of love more than it does its replaceable nature.

Take aways from this chapter:

1). To attract a healthy relationship, you must be healthy yourself.

2). It is possible to find love again and have a fruitful relationship.

3). The human heart is large enough to encompass more than one romantic love

12

Live with love and loss side by side

As far back as when I was a little child, I was fascinated by shadows.

Shadows are made by blocking light, where light rays travel from a source in straight lines. If a solid object gets in the way, it stops the rays from traveling through it. The size and shape of a shadow depend on the position and size of the light source compared to the object.

What I quickly learned is that shadows shrink and elongate and appear and disappear all the time. We see them clearly on floors, tables, and countertops when the sun bursts through a window and hits an opaque object in our homes. Buildings and architecture bounce light off their facades and create unique shadows in our cityscapes. The world stops and pauses to catch glimpses of our universe's more quintessential shadows through solar eclipses.

But if you were anything like me, your first experience with shadows happened when you were little, when your friends tried to draw your shape in the sand on dusty roads (I grew up in Africa) or trying to outrun your shadow (tell me I am not the only one who tried that).

I remember I would stand still while my brother drew my shadow in the ground and tell me it that I would have grown bigger or smaller later on. I would be so fascinated by my silhouette. Little did I know that I didn't grow much in those very short hours throughout the day, and it was more likely the sun's movement was the reason I either barely fit or completely outgrew the once near-perfect outline he would have drawn earlier.

As my brothers and I spent more time outdoors, I noticed the presence of shadows more and grew to appreciate their uniqueness even more. I recognised they were constantly there, and I couldn't miss them when conditions were ideal, but above all, we walk alongside them. With time I came to understand that even though shadows are intended to block light, the spinning of our earth on an axis means light can't touch every inch of earth all the time. As long as there is light, and we aren't translucent figures – even if we sometimes feel that way – darkness must also have its place.

When I finally comprehended this indirect, pivotal life lesson on equanimity, it was only then I understood why a grief journey, while excruciatingly painful at times, was also the reason I am whole. Because even though my experience with grief kept me feeling broken, battered, and a lot like that translucent skeleton hanging on by a heartbeat even I couldn't hear for years, the light somehow seemed to find a way to shine around me.

Because of my journey with grief, I have turned to writing and have taken to sharing my experiences of grieving with others not as a phycologist or grief expert but, as an individual sharing lived experiences.

In the spirit of honesty, even as I scribble this as a symbol of my victory and recognition of my journey with grief that could very well resurface in new ways later in life, it's been the hardest thing I've ever written to date. Recanting moments of loss and pain that revealed themselves in the past couple of years and sobbing uncontrollably throughout this wasn't just difficult, it was piercing. Forgiving my in-laws, who were not perfect and didn't always have the right approach to this journey of grief, was something I could do only after I realized what being human really meant and that I had to find it within myself to heal and accept my loss. Ultimately, forgiving myself – for all of the encounters or estranged behaviour I experienced around people I loved or cared about is something I still haven't fully achieved quite yet – but I've made tremendous progress.

It is important to give yourself permission for whatever you are experiencing. While others may be telling you to put it behind you and get on with life, I encourage you to build memories that you will never "put behind you". Healing does not mean forgetting; it means taking the life, love, and lessons into the future with you.

Eventually you are able to let go of what can no longer be. Yet at the same time you realize you are taking the past, with all its pain and pleasure, into a new tomorrow. You accommodate to the loss and assimilate it into your life. It becomes a treasured part of your story that helps you grow into a different and hopefully better, more compassionate, more appreciative, more tolerant person. Enriched by your past, you fully embrace life again, connecting, laughing, and loving with a full heart.

Pulling shadows out of your heart that have tried to disguise themselves as demons isn't just admirable, it's bravery – and it's that bravery that's finally allowed me to put this experience into words.

To anyone going through grief after loss of a loved one– you matter.

Your panic attacks don't make you a baby, weak, or feeble.

Your sensitivity provides you with keen and heightened awareness to small details people often forget, and that makes for a great partner or friend.

The grief you're experiencing from the loss of a loved one doesn't mean you will never feel whole again. You'll become a better listener, more spiritually attuned, more appreciative of life and the little things, and find ways to keep the memories of your loved one (and of your life) alive in unique ways.

The hopelessness and despair you can't explain but feel in the morning when you awake or in the moments just before bed don't mean you'll never find a way out. Those who feel emotions to their greatest negative intensities will eventually feel their positive opposites. You can only become receptive to receiving good energy quicker if you're honest about what it means to see the light.

In our world, especially these days, if we don't reimagine the definition of empathy to support people going through a period of grief, we are in all honesty inhumane.

As you walk through this grieving journey remember this.

Almost always, the light surrounding us is far superior to the speck of darkness that creates our shadows. We will always walk next to our shadow, your shadow, like the past is not your enemy. The memories of your loved ones are not something you can run from or close like a book you no longer want to read.

The mythical finish line of 'closure' is indeed, an invisible line. Do not chase that but instead learn to come to terms with your loss.

I have learned to walk with my shadow, I have come to an understanding that 'Closure' is like a mythical finish line.

There is no point at which you will never cry again, although as time goes on the tears are bittersweet and less common. Because you never forget, you carry your loved ones with you forever.

"Closure"? No, or at least not in the way people usually use that term. Acceptance – yes. Peace – yes. Moving forward – for sure. A future bright with love, joy, and hope – absolutely. But putting a period behind the final sentence, closing the door and locking it behind you? No. Love lives on and memories sing through the symphony that forms our lives.

The only way to transcend loss and grief is by learning to live with love and loss side by side.

You can't run from your shadow. I learnt that lesson as a little boy.

Take aways from this chapter:

1). To anyone going through grief after loss of a loved one– you matter.

2). Those who feel emotions to their greatest negative intensities will eventually feel their positive opposites.

3). You can only become receptive to receiving good energy quicker if you're honest about what it means to see the light.

4). The memories of your loved ones are not something you can run from or close like a book you no longer want to read.

13

Life is so unpredictable, never take your health for granted

Life is so unpredictable. Things happen suddenly, unexpectedly. We want to feel we are in control of our own existence. In some ways we are, in some ways we're not. We are ruled by the forces of chance and coincidence.

Most often than not, we take things for granted and we never realize that life is too short until a moment passes by.

It may sound cliche, but life is too fragile to take things, people, and moments for granted. This is why we should appreciate everything before life takes away everything we treasure, whether that's the people we love, places we've been to, or memories.

Life is indeed too short to not focus on the present moment and live it the best way we can.

A week after my birthday I woke up with plans to edit a few chapters and write a few more lines to my manuscript (new project sequel) to Grief Sucks But Hope Again.

Then I realised my thighs and knees which have been swelling up in the past few days were giving me discomfort.

I called 111 got an emergency appointment with my GP and after a few minutes with me she referred me to Acute Medical Unit at Princess Royal Hospital in Telford.

This is the same hospital that my wife died.

I thought well I will just be going in to get my blood test, scans and X-rays and I will be done.

I was not expecting what then came I was sent to the same ward that Tshidz's was put in.

And I kid you not it was so busy in AMU patients were seating in the corridor. I sat right outside the door to (side room 3) the very room I last spoke to Tshidz's 3 years ago.

One of the staff members from reception came to ask if my records needed updating. She causally asked, 'is your wife still your next of kin?'

It was at that moment that I realised this could be one of those situations that goes from a regular hospital visit to a serious thing. There was a chance I had a blood clot and that my life was in serious danger.

I was overwhelmed by emotions when one of the nurses (Casey) the sister in-charge who took care of Tshidz's came to speak to me. She recognised me and asked if I was okay. She asked how I have been since the passing of Tshidz's and asked about my son.

I was tearing up like a broken pipe. I had not been to this place since that fateful day more than 3 years ago.

She asked if I wanted to be put in a different place (given the memories and the emotions I attached to this place), she said she understood that the memories of this place would make me uncomfortable.

She was so kind, she sat with me comforted me and after a few minutes talking and a cup of tea later,

I told her about my book which she bought straight away on Amazon.

While I was in the hospital I reflected on a couple of things.

I realised; indeed, life is too short.

What 'Life is Too Short' Means

When you say life is too short, this means you shouldn't take the small things for granted. Every moment is so important so there's no use spending it being frustrated or angry about things you can't change. Life is fragile enough so take the opportunity to enjoy living, despite what situation you're in.

Whether it's the beauty of a sunrise or a cup of tea, enjoying the simple things is what this phrase is all about.

You stop wasting your time and energy on unnecessary things such as negativity and toxicity but rather, you embrace emotions such as gratitude and kindness. You know that a moment won't last, and you take advantage of being in that moment, while it hasn't passed just yet.

I know you might be wondering why I am talking about this in this book about 'closure' but that's me stressing the point we really do not have time to chase mythical finish lines.

We often overthink situations too much and deeply that we tend to lose focus on the reality in life – that life is too short and that we never know what the next day will bring – in some cases even the same day.

Life can change in a split second

One of the most common things that people have on their deathbeds is that they should have done more things and that life is short. When we are looking at our last few minutes on earth, we should be able to say that we lived a life worth living and that we enjoyed every bit of it without regrets.

These are some of the thoughts I reflected on while waiting for my hospital observations to be done and bloods drawn, and ultrasound scans done.

When they say life is too short, we often think about it, but never really take advantage of that fact. We say the quote and continue to do the things that we might not even want to do.

Do you think life is too short? If so, what are some of the things that you plan to do to make the best out of it?

Take aways from this chapter
Make a list of 3 things you plan to do make the best of the life you've got:

1).

2).

3).

"Closure" in grief

www.ingramcontent.com/pod-product-compliance
Lightning Source LLC
LaVergne TN
LVHW041234080426
835508LV00011B/1206